Calls From Home

Mystical Poems

Jakob Kaergaard

VitalUnit

Calls From Home
Published 2021 by VitalUnit

ISBN: 978-87-972826-1-8
vitalunit.com / jakobkaergaard.com

To Spirit, great and eternal,
and to my parents, who prepared
me well for this life

Contents

Preface	7
Life's Mystical Symphony	11
Full Freedom Is Now	13
I Am A Wine	15
Loving My Dark Side	16
Feel Me Now	17
The Origin Of Meaning	19
The Lord Comes To Everyone	20
Remember Me	22
The Great & The Small I	23
Enigma Of Dying	25
Armed With The Lord	27
My Religion Is The Greatest Of All	28
Mystical Cock	30
Ode To My Lady	32
The Scavenger & The Mirror	34
My Gift To Myself	35
Missing You	37
Beyond Labels	39
The Perils Of Full Freedom	40
The Purpose Of World History	42
My Entry Into This World	43
About The Author	45

Preface

February 2021
Lanzarote, Spain

On a day in early spring of 2017 I was climbing a mountain in Italy. It was a mountain I had been wanting to climb for 10 years while visiting the area. I had tried a few times before, sometimes alone sometimes with friends, but never managed due to changing weather conditions and losing our way. On this day I finally did it on my own. But something happened that day which I did not expect. I remember walking up the steep slopes of the mountain, about half way up, when I literally heard a voice speaking inside my head. It was so sudden and compelling that I stopped immediately, pulled out my phone and started writing down the words as I received them.

This became the first in a particular series of poems, a selection of which you'll find here on these pages. It is the second one in Calls From Home - 'Full Freedom Is Now'. The rest of them arrived at different times in the following three years, one on a flight going back to Italy a few months later, one at a cafe in Athens overshadowed by the Parthenon, one in my kitchen at home in my apartment in Denmark, and so on. Many of them have arrived pretty much in the form in which they now appear on these pages. Some emerged when pieces from these different transmissions 'glowed up' and seemed to fit together like pieces in a puzzle when I read them at a later stage.

Right since that first moment I have felt a compelling urge to share them. Like they wanted to get out and they chose me for that end. I also feel a certain presence behind them, even while writing this. Speaking them feels somewhat like a prayer, connecting me with that presence. It is sometimes strong, sometimes subtle, just as were the moments when they arrived. In some of those moments the voice was so subtle, like the gentlest presence calling me inwards. While at other times it felt like a roaring command. In each of these instances, the experience they most left me with was one of intimate connection with something much greater than myself. And a deep sense of belonging and a feeling of being home in this life and the world.

I hope you will enjoy these calls from home. May they inspire you on your journey through this mystery of existence. I also invite you to try to speak them to yourself or to a friend. They tend to come very much alive when they are spoken and shared.

Jakob Kærgaard

Life's Mystical Symphony

Life
You came to me once
And shone your breath into my being
While I rested as primordial bliss between the worlds
Loh! Then suddenly I had a body
The body of a man, proud, virile, erect
I laughed like a roaring thunder under the sky
I jolted from the Earth where I was conceived and sprang into existence

Life
Your only price for this new adventure is that you want to live everything through me!
Thus you gave me a strong and healthy body
A brilliant mind
A creative soul
And demanded me to use them
I accepted because I was frankly a bit bored
With the non-existence of pre-physical existence
And because you seduced me with such a forceful, loving gesture

Now I am here
And I vow to give my full Self to existence
Inviting everyone to equally receive me in my full Self

I declare every house and piece of land on this entire wide
Earth to be my home
I plant my flag in the heart of every human being
Life and I are preparing a great mystical symphony
We want you to be musician and audience alike
And we have only just begun

Full Freedom Is Now

The time has come
No need to wait any longer

I declare full freedom for humanity!

I rise from my simple bearing and brush eons of dust from off myself
I shout to you from out the desert and other wild and open places

You are free!

Your shackles fall off, also those you did not know that you wore
(they are by far the most numerous)
You stand quiet for a moment, aghast at this new won freedom
And then begin to tremor

Full freedom is terrible because it charges you with the task of making the best of your life
Many things are given, but you can always choose what to do with them
You can choose to accept your past and your destiny
While still making the best of any situation

That is the freedom I give you

It is also the freedom to be your full naked Self
Now finally in this age humans have the chance to be their full naked Selves
Without being burned or beheaded for their courage
At last we have come to this point
And I will accept nothing less of you!

Indeed, the tables have turned
Those who are fake, lying to themselves and the world
Those *I* will drag to the stake
Whatever is unreal
Appearing prettier and better than it is
I will happily submit to the flames

You can start the process yourself
Tidy up in your life
Before the tide of truth will engulf you
I have gifted you with a whole range of tools for this very purpose
They are all readily available in these times

Use them well and cleanse your Selves
Prepare them, make them fertile ground for my seeds
I have them in plenty and I long to sow the field of humanity
With new inspiration and bold ideas for a new world!

I Am A Wine

I am a Wine in a barrel
I am maturing
Don't disturb me or you will interrupt me in the process
Which could have disastrous consequences
Very soon you will be able to enjoy me
And you will get me at my best
When all my flavours have come together
And I will have my very own unique taste
Drink me then and enjoy
Let the sparkles of my inner world enchant you
But beware
Because like a catalyzing agent I will enter you
And begin your inner fermentation

Loving My Dark Side

I love my ego, or that which others call their ego
I love my faults and my shortcomings
My perversions and kinks
They are as fully a part of myself as my light
I penetrate into the darkest depths of my shadow
And acknowledge what I see
I know that I could annihilate the world given the worst circumstances
I also know that I could spawn an entire new Universe
Know and embrace the full depth of your shadow
Because that will be a measure of your light

Feel Me Now

I want you to feel me
Enough with your running away!
I am so sick of your endless excuses
Mortified by your ever more cunning ways of distracting yourself
I want your life, your blood, your vibrant presence
I want your gifts to existence - now!

Flee into your mind just one more time
And I will split your skull asunder
From the inside that is – cause that is where you'll find me
Hide within a healthy life style and I will send you some nasty disease
Cloud yourself in political correctness and I will find a way to smash your petty beliefs
They are like smoke
Grey, lifeless smoke that prevents you from seeing me clearly
They must be cleared from sight before our mutual play can begin

Beyond your armour of thought I am waiting for you
I was always waiting for you
Like the most faithful friend
The most dedicated lover

I am waiting for you
My heart bursts with anticipation when I imagine the day that you will come back to me
I know just what we will be doing – just come and I will whisper it in your ear

From that day on you & I will be creating a new universe
From that day on
Life will be worth Living
Once more

The Origin Of Meaning

Meaning is my gift to you
It is your divine pay check
I set it up like an automated system
So that it's issued automatically
Whenever you do what you're supposed to do
Oh yes, you have your free will
But even that is a gift from me
Because I want to feel that you come back to me out of true longing
Listen to me carefully
I will find you in your dreams when your mind's defenses are down
Or in the quiet moments that you can use your free will to create
Make yourself an empty vessel, and I will give you the inspiration that you're asking for
Nourish it within yourself, no matter how silly or insignificant it may seem
Live with it, create from it, and I promise
Meaning will originate for you

The Lord Comes To Everyone

The Lord comes to everyone at some stage in their lives
But not everyone wants to receive him
They are afraid of what he might have to tell them
They are afraid they might have to change their ways
And most likely they will
Most likely they will be taken on such a flight
They'll completely forget about themselves
And when they return be utterly uncomfortable with their old self

Then starts the long and arduous journey
Of molding that old self
Into something that can host the Lord
On a regular basis
And that is not easy
Particularly not when that old self of yours
Is a cracked old bucket full of trash and dog-poo
And most likely it is

But if that is the self you have
Then that is your starting point
Imagining anything finer than that
Will only keep your soul back at square one
While you go off fancying being enlightened

Be true with yourself!
Truth is the only virtue
That over time will transform that old bucket of yours
Along with its nasty interiors
Into a palace of gold
And then one day when you least expect it
The Lord will arrive again

You will feel him like a new presence within you
Yet a presence that you know
Like an itching stir at the core of your being
He will demand your attention
And your ears for the task he has to give you

Remember Me

At times when you get absorbed by the vicissitudes of life
Remember me
I am still there
I am still there as that voice
In the back of your head
Saying
I am
Yet not as a thought
And not as words in a language
But like a presence
A presence who's depths are far, far greater
Than anything that fills your mind in any given moment
Remember me
You were born out of me
And you will return to me
Again

The Great & The Small I

Sometimes I am the great I
Sometimes I am the small
I have no problem being both of them
I know that I am both of them

I can be so small you could squeeze me dead
Between the tips of your fingers
Like a baby bird cuddling up against your chest
I can be so vast you'd be completely without words
To fathom or describe me
A welder of stars, inspirator of prophets, ignitor of universes

But I am more

I am the cream on your birthday cake
On the happiest birthday of your life
I am the love you hide in your heart
And that chance encounter
That shapes the rest of your life

I am the weapon of your enemy
that saps your life force
And the hands of the healer that cures you
I am your mother's agony

As she pushes you into this world

I am your wonder and bewilderment
As you ponder the purpose of life
I am that bubbling joy which you find pulsing
Spontaneously through your being

All of this I am - and yet more
I am beyond any experience and expression of space-time

I am a disembodied smile in the emptiness
I am the rich, sweet fullness of subatomic space
I am that which was and which wasn't
That which is coming and that which shall never be born

With a Self like this - how to even exist in human form?
It is not easy - and the truth is
That I don't
And neither do you

Enigma Of Dying

I'm ready to die
Ready to be blown to pieces
Crushed, crucified, intestines pulled from my body
My brain hacked to pieces and fed to some starving divinity

I'm ready to let it all go
Living fully from moment to moment
So strongly that nothing remains ungiven when finally I let go

I die every single day
Letting go of a new - or rather an old
Part of myself
Which I no longer am
Being born every morning
Embracing the new
Which yesterday's death has revealed

I love death
I celebrate death
Death makes me free
Brings me closer to that which I am

I am an artist of dying
I know how to die in my mind

Without needing to kill my physical vessel

So much time can be saved that way
So much future existence
Letting die what needs to
Letting live what has impetus to live

Death enables me to love
When I die onto myself
I become free
When I am free
I can truly love
When I truly love
I unify with existence

That should be plenty to make this life a meaningful one

Armed With The Lord

Armed with the Lord I am
Yet vulnerable as the sea
Hit me with anything
And I will give way
Entrust me with Life
And I will make it flourish
I love you
I love you
Come hither
And I will dissolve you
In my bosom

My Religion Is The Greatest Of All

My religion is the greatest of all and yet I need no priests or sacred books
Nature is my sacred book
In it I see the light of God governing the very motion of the stars
And in my garden the spurs of the butterflies
I read my sacred poems in the eyes of my brothers and sisters
I see divine humour in the kinks and tweaks of their personalities
Their jests, their apt bodies
They are all expressions of God
Even the god-deniers are expressions of God
Their most vehement attack on the existence of God is a beautiful divine expression of cunning argument

The scientists do their calculations
They formulate their theories
They write God out of their account of the cosmos
But do they really think they know what a law of nature is just by putting it on an equation?
What is actually a law of nature?
Why is it there?
Why are there gravity, electromagnetism, and the forces that bind the nucleus together?

Why aren't there just formless plasma?
Why aren't there just absolutely nothing?
Give me the scientist who can answer that question and I will show you a prophet in disguise

I will tell you what the laws of nature are
They are God's will bending the universe
God has been doing so since the very beginning
And has been experimenting with other laws of nature in countless other universes
Some with less of a lucky result
You see, God is not omnipotent
It sure may seem so to us
But God is still conquering this universe of form
Testing, playing, experimenting
Manifesting its divine potential in every shape and form
And we are soldiers in the front line of that magnificent experiment

Mystical Cock

I come in many forms throughout the ages
In this one I came with a magnificent cock
It is because your age is so dense and meaty
You guys revel so much in your lower instincts that I have to meet you there
In every dimension of existence there is a path to me
So if you are governed by your passion and desires that is where you must find me

My cock is the bridgehead to all mysticism
The entrypoint to the underworld
It is the spearhead of my Self
A vital elongation of my Being
With it I will give you my greatest gift
An imprint of my Self
To be diffused in the waters of your soul
In time my seed will reach your Self
And activate you like a long-lost satellite that comes within the range of the Earth
Your central core will illuminate itself
And your most ancient parts feel the flow of life once more

Woman, open the portal for me
Let your body become the instrument that can take us both to the beyond

With my potent presence and sacred cock I shall adorn your offering
And activate the mystical gateway that you are
Woman, did you know?
You have the capacity to bring any man to his fullest flowering
If you choose to submit to that role and he chooses to grow through the challenge
Then he can become that mystical key that opens your portal
But it takes training, long and arduous training
And a strong yet tender heart, dedicated to truth

Ode To My Lady

Lady
Your womanhood fills me with awe
Your dance mesmerizes my being
Your scent makes me vigilant like a deer smelling its mate
And a tiger sensing its prey

I dive headlong into the universe that is your eyes
Dying to explore every nick and cranny of your landscape
I want to know everything that you contain
I want to dance in your rivers
Get drunk on your nectar
Scale your highest mountain
Conquer your golden city
Burn myself in your volcanic fires and rise again like a phoenix from my ashes
Ready to penetrate your deepest forest
And prostrate myself
In humble prayer
In front
Of your sacred
Temple

Lady, rip me open
And fill me with your gifts
Your light, your love, your tenderness

Your desire, wrath, sweetness, life
And with your mystery
Your knight and lover is here
I want to know the universe through you
And I will not hold back until I do

The Scavenger & The Mirror

I'm a scavenger
I feed on the abandoned fragments of dead human souls
I am hungry!
Eager as hell to draw them into me and make them part of myself
To digest and absorb them and enlarge myself in the process
That is what I do
Scouring through the vile debris of humanity's astral graveyard
Looking for some juicy piece of soul to put my teeth in
It's a dubious undertaking and some high-minded souls perpetually let me feel their scorn
But they are stupid
Because what I really mean to do
Is to unite one fraction of the divine mirror within myself

My Gift To Myself

Life and the world is my gift to myself
I conjured up this spectacular marvel to seduce and delight myself
I designed the fabric of existence to be strong enough to hold it all together
Yet permeable to the mystic's eye
I took care to build mortality into existence
Without which evolution would have been impossible
And to make sure I had an exit route for myself

I also took care to build plenty of difference into existence
Thus I created man and woman, night and day
Predator and prey, happiness and depression
The greater and more numerous the differences
The greater the variety of expression
And that is why I came here!
I came to amuse myself
In the bliss-worlds all is uniform bliss
But here I can have a multitude of experience!

So play for me existence!
Dance for me dear spectacle, and throw up the most exotic of your creations
The most bizarre combinations of the pre-conceived differences

I want to see them all!
I know that they are but a shadow of my true being
And there are moments where I find this inherently delightful
And moments where it bores me to death
But that is but the nature of existence

I also decided to humble myself
That is also why I took on this form
Yes I created the universe
And designed this human game
Who would I then be to not take part in it myself
I am here with you, living and dying with you
Feeling all the throes of conflicting emotions
The loss of loved ones, the burden of being alive
Experiencing the confusion and meaninglessness
That is part and parcel of human existence
Let me tell you, when you've been steeped in the bliss-realms for long enough
Even that can become a torture
And a bit of boredom and meaninglessness the ultimate bliss
At the end of a long succession of lives
The souls just long to dissolve themselves in my being
But I, my dear ones, long for you
Which is why I keep on coming back to you time and again

Missing You

I'm flowing through life
Like the rest of you
Not knowing where I am going
Or where it will end
Or what the fuck I am doing here in the first place
The good thing is
I don't need to know
I need to know absolutely nothing
I don't care where I come from
Or what happens with my consciousness when I die
How my Self was forged
Or how the surrounding universe came into being
I fathom it emerged from the depths of my own soul
Or convoluted itself from my last eye contact with you,
My love
It isn't really that important
What is important is that I miss you
As I have missed you ever since you lost yourself in form
That day in some remote, unmentionable past
I know you don't remember it
But I have watched you diligently ever since
Upholding the space around you as you move
Silently listening to your troubled thoughts
Hoping that one day you will notice my presence
When you do we will be ready to make the world real again

Instead of just some random fluctuation in the quantum field
Then indeed we shall know where we are going
And remember why we were here to begin with

Beyond Labels

Put a label on me if you dare
I will shatter it with a vengeance
I am beyond your labels
I am your most cherished ideal and most horrible nightmare
I am a God of fuck
A warrior of love
A child in a flowergarden
A princess at her wedding ceremony
I am that which is living and that which is dead
I am your trauma and your therapist
Your seducer and your desire
I am your deepest, innermost longing
Come back to me
Come back to me
I have had enough of silly games

The Perils Of Full Freedom

There is something I haven't told you
Full freedom is perilous
Because when the shackles imposed on you
By your culture, your parents, and your self
Are removed
All of your inner demons will be set free
And be yours to deal with
 - and for most of you that is indeed a mighty task

I'm aware it did not exactly say that on the declaration
But I'm afraid there is nothing to do at this point
The elixir of freedom is active in Humanity
And it will do its magic on all of you
Some of you will take longer to soften up
But the time will come for you all

When it happens I advice you to take them one at a time
Deal with your personal demons first
And remember to take some breaks in between
If you manage well there are plenty of dragons in the deep
Karma from your family, your culture and past existences
That needs to be distilled and the gold and gems from
them extracted

It is a momentous task I have given you - I know that

A major work that only happens once in many ages
I also know that some of you will break under it
Some of you will be devoured by your monsters
Who next will turn to devour the people you love -
through you

I'm sad about this, but there really is no other way
Humanity must rise now or plunge into the shadows
But I believe in you - I know that you will succeed
You will manage taming your demons
Turning them into the allies they were always meant to be
And that will be worth the sacrifice

It is time to clean the house of Humanity
I have given you that job
Some of you will fail and I accept the full responsibility
Those of you who make it can keep the glory for yourselves

The Purpose Of World History

It may not appear so from the inside
But world history has been an attempt to unite Myself
It's been a rather messy affair, I know
Sometimes that was part of the purpose
Sometimes there were some mishaps
You see, I know you'd like to think I've got it all under control
It makes me laugh like a thunder under the Heavens!
I'm playing
With you, me and all of us
Attempting to find a way where the great and the small can come together
Where differences can remain yet be bridged
Where I can finally achieve a feeling of oneness within form
Such a hard work it is
And you guys certainly don't make it easy
Stiff and stubborn as you are
You resist my attempts to guide you
Which is why I sometimes have to be a bit hard on you
Don't take it personally though
It is all for the sake of the greater mission
And you shall know my love for you is boundless
Like the Universe

My Entry Into This World

I realized today that I did not negotiate my entry into this world with God
I negotiated it with myself
I chose to be born
I chose the path taken with every peril and delight
I accepted the full plan that I was presented with
By myself
I could have stayed where I was in primordial bliss
Enjoying the timeless fruits of being
But I chose to accept the challenge
That I created for myself
Because I thought it would be fun

About The Author

Jakob works as a men's coach, specializing in male sexuality, life purpose and what it means to be a man. He is the creator of the Vital Force Sexual Mastery program, that teaches men the key techniques to master their sexual energy. This is a practise that leads to increased energy levels, cures most sexual dysfunctions for men, creates greater pleasure and intimacy, and can lead to expanded states of awareness during sex.

In his own life, he has spent a lot of time exploring what it means to be a man. This has led him to define the 12 steps towards becoming a man - a series of steps and challenges that will be key for any man, no matter his cultural and social background or status, wanting to build a mature, male self.

Jakob holds a master's degree in philosophy and history. You can read more about his work at vitalunit.com and jakobkaergaard.com.

Printed in Great Britain
by Amazon

10334012R00031